S0-BAT-279

A TINY FISH
TALE

Written and Illustrated by Lois Ivancin Tavaf

thanks for contributing to this
great cause!

Lois Ivancin Tavaf

My name is Simon.

I live in California.

I have 2 bulldogs, Lilly Belle and Ox.

My Grandma and Grandpa had a really big wolfhound for their pet when they lived in Wisconsin.

Her name was Tatiana.

She had a lot of room to play and enjoyed the cold weather.

When Grandma and Grandpa moved to Washington, DC, they could not have a big dog in their small place.

My cousin Will, who lives near them, convinced them to get a pretty little betta fish.

He is the size of my pinky finger.

Grandma and Grandpa
read all about how to care
for a fish, and prepared
their place for his arrival.

They got a big and tall fish bowl, and put some fancy live plants to float on the top of the water and put a few on the bottom of the bowl.

Fish like real plants in their bowl.

They put a little two-story stone house for the fish to hide in and feel safe.

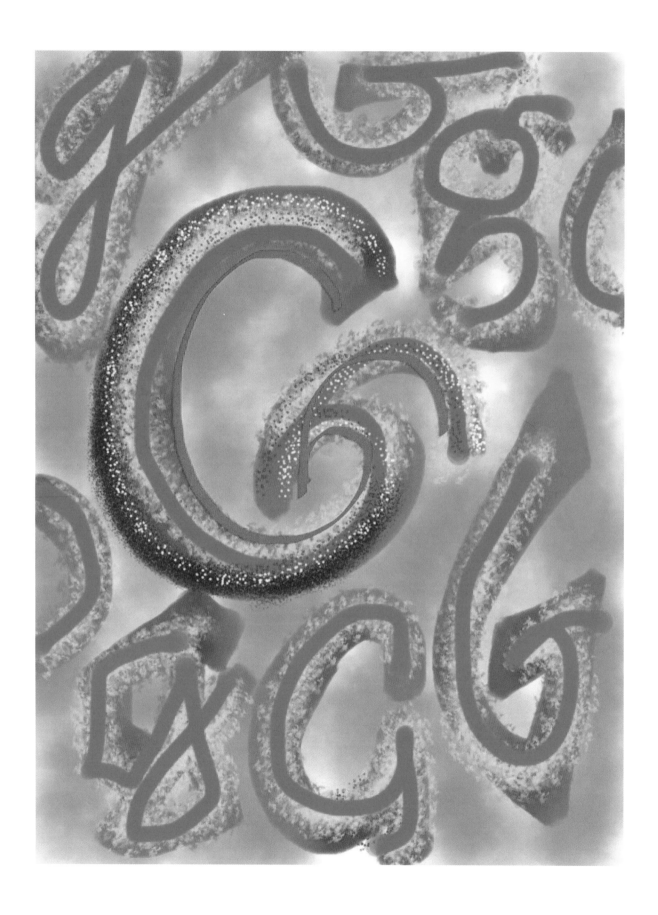

Grandma and Grandpa named the fish "G," which is short for "GW," which is even shorter for George Washington.

I asked them "why did you name him George Washington?"

They told me they had a contest on Facebook and this was the winning entry.

Plus, they really love George Washington.

G was shy the first few days.

He hid in his house a lot.

But he was also hungry.

So G came to the surface looking for the fish food that Grandma and Grandpa sprinkled on the water.

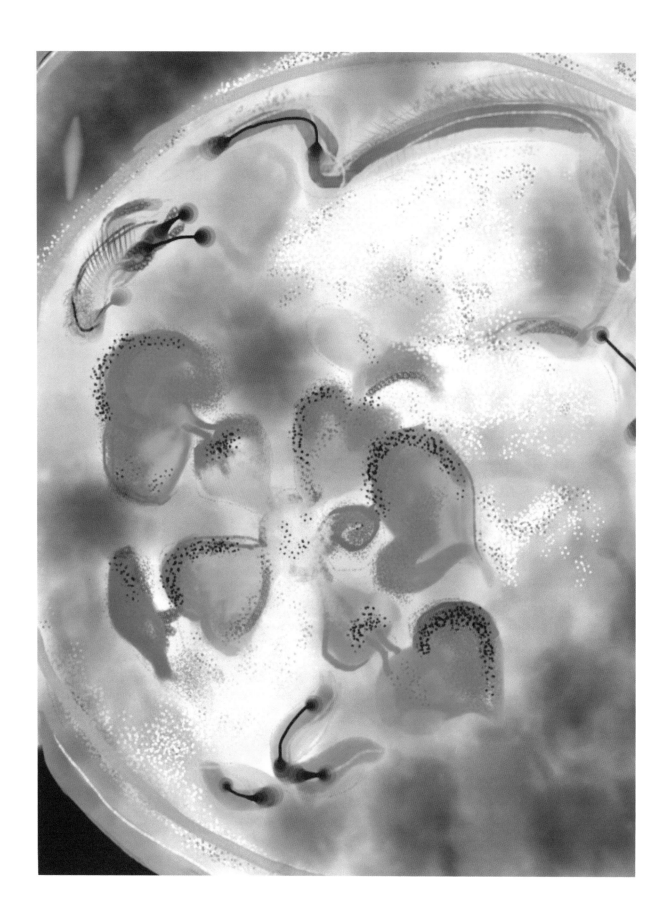

Grandma and Grandpa told me that G would dance when you waved at him.

He would blow bubbles.

He saw himself in a mirror and liked what he saw!

G changed colors from blue to red when the sunlight was on him.

Grandpa changed the water in his bowl every week.

My cousin Will would feed
G if Grandma and
Grandpa went out of
town.

G was a very happy little
fish.

One day, G wasn't moving around very much.

He was tired all the time and did not eat anymore.

One of his eyes looked like it popped out!

Grandma and Grandpa did not know what to do.

They read about what caused the "pop-eye" on the internet and asked their friends for help.

They learned that these fish, like any living thing, are sensitive to changes in their environment and might get sick.

So they changed the water more frequently and very carefully.

They put less water in the bowl so G would not have to swim so far to reach the top.

They put medicine in his water.

They talked to him.

Nothing seemed to help.

Everyone asked Grandma and Grandpa...."why are you keeping G?"

His other eye popped out.

He could not see himself
in the mirror.

He could not see the food
to eat.

G could not see anymore!

Grandpa thought G may
not get better if he could
not see and did not eat.

It was a sad day...

Grandma thought there must be a way to get G to eat even if he could not see.

They had to try!

The experts said these fish are strong.

Don't give up!

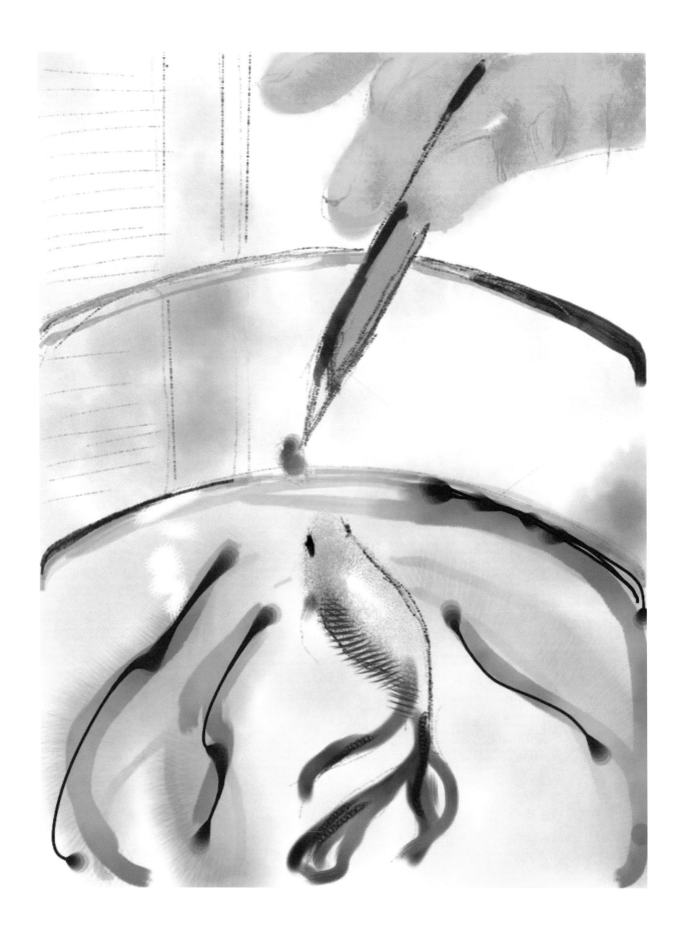

Grandma got a pair of tweezers and attached some food to the end of it.

She tapped on the side of the bowl and called to G.

She tapped again, and called him again.

She tapped, and tapped.

G finally heard her call
and tapping and swam to
the top of the bowl.

Grandma put the food
near his mouth with the
tweezers.

G felt the food, but did
not know what to do.
Grandma put the food
again next to G's mouth.

Finally!

After many tries, G
figured out it was food
and gulped it down!

Could Grandma train him
to eat again even though
G could not see?

Grandma and Grandpa
called G every day and fed
him.... Day after day.

G started to perk up.

He began to move about the bowl, but he still could not see.

He bumped into the plants, and floated down to the bottom of the bowl in a free fall.

Grandma and Grandpa realized that G might not recover and was blind forever.

Even though G could not see, he started to learn to glide through the water and swim around the plants.

He started to lay on the plant leaves and rest.

He started to flap his fins when he heard his name - just like before he was sick.

G looks like a regular fish now.

Sometimes he even sits on the top of his house.

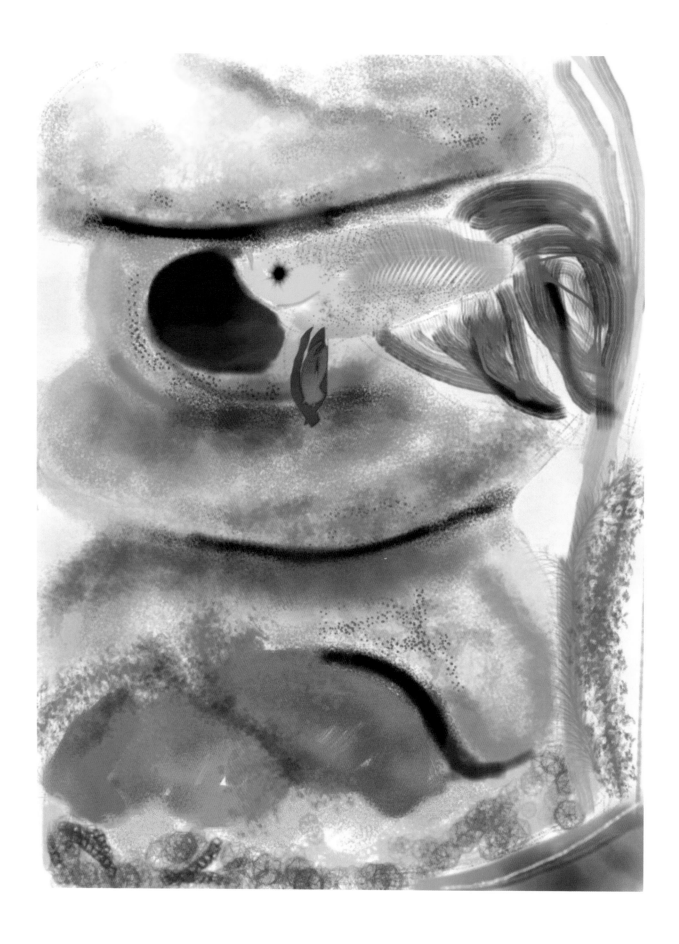

I'm so happy that Grandma and Grandpa cared for G when he needed it the most.

G is happy Grandma and Grandpa took such good care of him too!

And guess what I am going to do?

21487771R00037

Made in the USA
Charleston, SC
19 August 2013